# DODD, MEAD WONDERS BOOKS

*Wonders of the Mosquito World by Phil Ault*
*Wonders of the World of Bears by Bernadine Bailey*
*Wonders of Animal Migration by Jacquelyn Berrill*
*Wonders of Animal Nurseries by Jacquelyn Berrill*
*Wonders of the Arctic by Jacquelyn Berrill*
*Wonders of the Monkey World by Jacquelyn Berrill*
*Wonders of the Woods and Desert at Night by Jacquelyn Berrill*
*Wonders of the World of Wolves by Jacquelyn Berrill*
*Wonders of Alligators and Crocodiles by Wyatt Blassingame*
*Wonders of Frogs and Toads by Wyatt Blassingame*
*Wonders of a Kelp Forest by Joseph E. Brown*
*Wonders of Rattlesnakes by G. Earl Chace*
*Wonders of the Pelican World by Joseph J. Cook and Ralph W. Schreiber*
*Wonders Inside You by Margaret Cosgrove*
*Wonders of the Tree World by Margaret Cosgrove*
*Wonders of Your Senses by Margaret Cosgrove*
*Wonders of Wild Ducks by Thomas D. Fegely*
*Wonders Beyond the Solar System by Rocco Feravolo*
*Wonders of Gravity by Rocco Feravolo*
*Wonders of Mathematics by Rocco Feravolo*
*Wonders of Sound by Rocco Feravolo*
*Wonders of the World of the Albatross by Harvey I. and Mildred L. Fisher*
*Wonders of the World of Shells by Morris K. Jacobson and William K. Emerson*
*Wonders of Animal Architecture by Sigmund A. Lavine*
*Wonders of the Bat World by Sigmund A. Lavine*
*Wonders of the Cactus World by Sigmund A. Lavine*
*Wonders of the Eagle World by Sigmund A. Lavine*
*Wonders of the Fly World by Sigmund A. Lavine*
*Wonders of the Hawk World by Sigmund A. Lavine*
*Wonders of the Owl World by Sigmund A. Lavine*
*Wonders of the Spider World by Sigmund A. Lavine*
*Wonders of the World of Horses by Sigmund A. Lavine and Brigid Casey*
*Wonders of the Bison World by Sigmund A. Lavine and Vincent Scuro*
*Wonders of Magnets and Magnetism by Owen S. Lieberg*
*Wonders of Measurement by Owen S. Lieberg*
*Wonders of the Dinosaur World by William H. Matthews III*
*Wonders of Fossils by William H. Matthews III*
*Wonders of Sand by Christie McFall*
*Wonders of Stones by Christie McFall*
*Wonders of Gems by Richard M. Pearl*
*Wonders of Rocks and Minerals by Richard M. Pearl*
*Wonders of Barnacles by Arnold Ross and William K. Emerson*
*Wonders of Seagulls by Elizabeth and Ralph Schreiber*
*Wonders of Hummingbirds by Hilda Simon*

# Wonders of Sea Gulls

### Elizabeth Anne
### and
### Ralph W. Schreiber

ILLUSTRATED WITH PHOTOGRAPHS
BY THE AUTHORS

*With our best wishes*
*Anne*
*Betty*
*Ralph W. Schreiber*

DODD, MEAD & COMPANY · NEW YORK

IN MEMORY OF
Robert Watt Ferguson
who would have shared so well with us the wonders of this world

ACKNOWLEDGMENTS

Appreciation is expressed to William H. Drury and the Massachusetts Audubon Society; Robert L. DeLong and Robert L. Pyle of the Pacific Ocean Biological Survey Program; the Frank M. Chapman Fund of the American Museum of Natural History; the International Council for Bird Preservation; Boston Whaler, Inc.; Outboard Marine Corporation; the St. Petersburg Audubon Society; Rosemary Casey; Jan Cook; A. P. W. Connelly; James J. Dinsmore; Anne Ferguson; Dr. and Mrs. William I. Schreiber; and Bill Ward.

PICTURE CREDITS

Photos courtesy of: David Ainley, page 65; USFWS, J. C. Bartonek, page 22; Ted Lewin, page 41. All other photographs are by the authors. Drawings are by Elizabeth Anne Schreiber.

**Library of Congress Cataloging in Publication Data**
Schreiber, Elizabeth Anne.
  Wonders of sea gulls.

  SUMMARY: Discusses the characteristics and behavior of this symbol of life at sea and describes some of the more common species found in the northern hemisphere.
  Includes index.
  1. Gulls—Juvenile literature. [1. Gulls]
I. Schreiber, Ralph W., joint author. II. Title.
QL696.C46S35      598.3'3      75-11437
ISBN 0-396-07200-3

# Contents

*A laughing gull gets a running start for a take-off*

# I

## The Versatile, Social Sea Gull

Sea gulls soaring amidst the clouds or dipping down to snatch a meal from the water have long been envied by man in his desire to fly. The sea gull has always been an adventuresome symbol of life at sea. Most sea gulls, as their name implies, live near the sea at some time in their lives. However, some species in the sea-gull family live inland and are never near salt water. Thus the name "sea gull" is not always correct. "Gull" is a better general or common name for them.

These graceful white and gray birds with their black markings are one of the most commonly seen and recognized groups of birds. This is because many gulls show little fear of man. They spend considerable time in areas inhabited by humans. One reason that gulls live near humans is the food provided by man. Gulls find areas such as garbage dumps and dirty harbors and bays good places to feed. The inland gulls frequently search for insects in fields being plowed by farmers.

Very rarely is a gull seen flying or feeding by itself. Gulls spend most of their time with other members of their species and thus are called "social" birds. During the breeding season, generally lasting from March through August, gulls nest in colonies varying in size from a few to twenty thousand pairs. They

*Sociable laughing gulls don't mind sharing their feeding area with other shore birds.*

build their nests on flat sandy places along seashores, on islands, around inland lakes, or in marshes. Some gull species, such as ivory gulls and kittiwakes, nest on the ledges of buildings or on cliffs. But whatever the landscape, gulls always nest near other members of their own species. Other birds often nest with the gulls. Cormorants, terns, and ducks do this.

Usually gulls feed in flocks. A feeding flock may be composed of as few as five gulls or as many as five thousand. When one gull finds a source of food, it dives downward, giving a loud call and flashing its white underparts. This signals to nearby gulls that food has been found. Soon the air is filled with screaming, darting birds, eagerly feeding.

Gulls also roost and loaf in communal flocks. Each day as the sun sets, the gulls take off, a few at a time, and fly away from their feeding areas. They land on a sand bar, an open field, or calm water, where they roost for the night, relatively safe from predators. Loafing is what gulls do in the daytime when they are not busy feeding. The local gull inhabitants of an area normally have a favorite spot or two where a few members of their species may always be found loafing. Gulls use their loafing time to preen their feathers, rest or sleep. Roosting and loafing spots tend to be large open areas where the gulls can easily see any potential danger approaching.

Gulls even migrate together, usually in small and loosely formed groups. They rarely migrate in large flocks. Gulls of the northern hemisphere straggle along the coasts or through inland areas toward the south in the fall. In the southern hemisphere, gulls tend to head north after the breeding season is over, although most of them don't go a great distance. As warm weather and long days return in the spring, the gulls start toward their breeding grounds.

*Herring gulls loafing in a pasture in Maine*

Migration is probably a response to food shortage. When the lakes and bays freeze over in the winter, food becomes hard to find. Those individuals that move to warmer climates find food more easily and survive. The ones that do not migrate do not survive.

Being a social group, gulls, like humans, need to communicate with one another, whether in defending a territory, claiming a mate, or warning each other of danger. They do this by using their bodies and voices in what ornithologists (scientists who study birds) call "displays." A display is a set of movements

*Two displaying gulls face each other and defend their territories.*

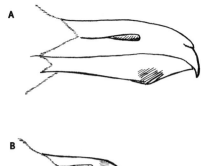

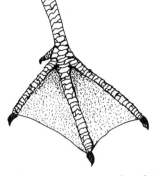

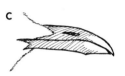

*Left: Comparison of the bills of three gulls: A, Great black-backed; B, Ring-billed; and C, Bonaparte's. Drawn to scale.*
*Above: The foot of a laughing gull, typical of all gulls, with three toes connected by a web and the fourth toe much smaller.*

of the body, often combined with certain calls. Each display communicates an important message to other gulls. Niko Tinbergen, a Dutch biologist, won the 1973 Nobel Prize in medicine for his work on herring-gull communication. Each gull inherently knows the displays used by his species without having to be taught what they mean. Gulls are very noisy birds and much of their behavior is accompanied by loud, harsh calls.

The different species of gulls range in length from 10 to 32 inches. In spite of this great variety in size, all gulls look and behave remarkably alike. They have sturdy, robust bodies. Their wings are a generalized shape—wide, long, and pointed at the tip. This wing shape enables gulls to fly equally well by flapping, soaring, or gliding. Most species of birds are specifically adapted for only one of these forms of flying.

Gulls' bills are stout and slightly down-curved at the tip. Their legs are three to seven inches in length. Gulls weigh from one-half to five pounds. Their feet are webbed, with the three inner toes connected by the web. The fourth toe is directed backward and is very small. There is a short, not very sharp claw on the end of each toe. Male and female gulls are alike in plumage and color. Males are often larger than females but this difference is difficult to see. Gulls may live to be as old as twenty-five years in the wild.

Gulls are good swimmers, bobbing along buoyantly on top of the water. Their feathers insulate them from the cold and wet. They propel and guide themselves with their webbed feet. Gulls can fly skillfully in all kinds of weather, and they walk about easily on dry land. Few birds can walk, swim, *and* fly as well as the gulls.

One of the most versatile birds known to man, gulls have evolved so they can readily adapt to different situations. When man builds houses in a gull nesting colony, the gulls find another place to nest. If one food source is used up or disappears, they move on and find another. In recent times, many species of birds have become extinct because the habitat in which they lived changed and they could not adapt to the new conditions. This has not happened to the gulls. So far they have been able to survive in our rapidly changing environment.

Perhaps this great versatility and adaptability will enable gulls to continue to survive in man's ever-changing world.

# II

## Meet the Gulls

There are forty-four different species of gulls in the world. Some make their homes in cold climates and others live in warm climates. They are seen from the Arctic to the Antarctic. Most beaches of all continents throughout the world have gulls present at some time during the year, and these birds are found at some time during the year in every state in the United States.

Some gull species are among the most well-studied birds in the world. Other species, especially those living in areas isolated from man, have received little attention. The gulls mentioned in the following pages are selected from some of the more common and well-studied Laridae of the northern hemisphere.

### GLAUCOUS GULL — *Larus hyperboreus*
Glaucous gulls are circumpolar breeders. This means that they nest near or within the Arctic Circle on islands or on the northern parts of continents. After the glaucous gulls finish raising their young in the short arctic summer, they migrate south in the fall to the British Isles, north-central Europe, the coasts of Japan and China, and into the northern United States coasts and the Great Lakes, occasionally as far south as Georgia or Texas.

They are one of the largest gull species, varying in size from 29 to 31 inches in length. Their wing span is about 60 inches. The outer edges of the wing feathers on glaucous gulls are white, while the rest of the wings are light gray. As with most gulls, the tail, head, and underparts are all white. Their bills are almost all yellow with some flesh color at the base. The legs are pinkish.

### GREAT BLACK-BACKED GULL — *Larus marinus*

These gulls are the same size as glaucous gulls, both weighing about five pounds. They breed primarily on islands along the coasts of the northeastern United States, Greenland, Labrador, Newfoundland, Iceland, Scotland, northern Europe, and east into Russia. Great black-backs arrive at their breeding places in early spring. In late August they begin to migrate south along the coasts and to southern inland lakes. This species is greatly expanding its range in the United States and only in recent years have they wintered as far south as Florida. The numbers

*The immature great black-backed gull has black-, brown-, and white-spotted back and wings. Its tail is black.*

are increasing in the southeastern states each year as the total population increases in the northeast. Elsewhere in the world the great black-backs winter throughout northern Europe and south to the Mediterranean and Caspian seas.

Great black-backs get their name from their large size and dark, slate gray back and wings. There is some white along the outer edge of the wings and the rest of the body is white. They have yellow legs. The bill is yellow with a red spot on the lower mandible.

### WESTERN GULL — *Larus occidentalis*
Large numbers of western gulls are seen along the coasts of Washington, California, Baja California, and the Gulf of California throughout the year. They are 17 to 19 inches in length and have dark gray backs and wings. Western and great black-backed gulls are similar in appearance. The best way to tell them apart is by size and distribution. They are not generally

*An adult western gull looks similar to but is smaller than the great black-backed gull. Their ranges do not overlap.*

found in the same areas.

Western gulls probably migrate the shortest distance of any of the gulls. They concentrate near their breeding areas on islands along the western United States and Mexican coasts in the spring and summer. In the fall and winter, they disperse away from the nesting colonies to feed and loaf along the coast.

### HERRING GULL — *Larus argentatus*

Herring gulls range from 23 to 24 inches in length. They have gray backs and wings with black wing tips. Great black-backs and herring gulls are frequently found together, searching for food, roosting, and nesting. It is fairly easy to tell them apart since herring gulls have lighter gray backs and are smaller.

Herring gulls are the most widely distributed gull species of

*An adult herring gull eyes the photographer. The spot on the tip of the lower mandible is red.*

the Western Hemisphere. They breed near the coasts from Alaska through Greenland, the northern British Isles to Sweden and northern Russia, and south into British Columbia, Minnesota, New York, and along the eastern seaboard to Virginia. They migrate south in the winter, often just far enough to find unfrozen waters in which to feed, but they are also seen as far south as Central America, southern United States, Africa, India, the Philippines, the Canary Islands, and the Black and Caspian seas.

## CALIFORNIA GULL — *Larus californicus*

California gulls breed in the inland plains of the United States and Canada. They range throughout the Great Plains from northern California and Utah north to the Arctic. These gulls usually avoid areas inhabited by man, so little is known about their distribution and numbers. Their fall migration takes them west and southwest from the breeding grounds. They are common on the west coast of the United States, south from southern Washington and through the Gulf of California to Guatemala during the winter. In April they head back to the Plains and build their nests around inland lakes.

California gulls are similar in size to western gulls. They can be told apart by the lighter gray backs and black wing tips of the california gulls.

## RING-BILLED GULL — *Larus delawarensis*

Years ago this gull was so common that John James Audubon called it the "common American gull." It is apparently much less abundant today. Man has moved into many of its former breeding areas and these gulls now nest in only a few areas of the interior of North America.

Ring-bills breed primarily in southern Canada, and from New York State across the northern states to central Washing-

ton. In the fall they head southeast or southwest to winter on the Atlantic or Pacific coasts, depending on where they nested previously. Some are seen as far south as Cuba, and they also migrate to the Gulf of Mexico. In March and April they move inland and north again.

Ring-bills are about 17 inches in length, and their wing span is almost four feet. Their backs and wings are gray and there are black markings on the wing tips. Legs and bills are yellow and there is a black ring around the tip of the bill.

*Above: A young ring-billed gull soars overhead in search of food.*

*The adult ring-billed gull is considerably smaller than the herring gull, although the two appear very similar. There is a black ring around the tip of the ring-billed gull's bill.*

## Laughing Gull —*Larus atricilla*

Laughing gulls nest from Nova Scotia south along the Atlantic and Gulf of Mexico coasts to Texas, eastern Mexico, and the Bahama Islands. They also nest in the Salton Sea of California and along the west coast of Mexico. Their numbers have increased importantly in recent years in the northeastern United States. The breeding season lasts from April through August for

*Black hood indicates the breeding plumage of adult laughing gull. Laughing, franklin's and bonaparte's gulls all look very much alike.*

laughing gulls. In September these 16-inch-long gulls begin to move south for the winter, from southern Mexico to northern Peru on the west coast, and from North Carolina throughout the Gulf of Mexico, the Carribean Sea, and as far south as the Amazon Delta.

It is believed that laughing gulls get their name from one of their calls, which sounds like a series of low chuckles. Their

*The laughing gull has all black tips on the outer primary wing feathers.*

wing tips are solid black with the rest of the wings and backs gray. The legs and bills are black. During the breeding season both turn a deep shade of red to varying extents, depending on the individual bird.

### Franklin's Gull — *Larus pipixcon*

Franklin's gulls were considered rare until man explored the inland areas of the United States and discovered them breeding there in large numbers. They are slightly smaller than laughing gulls, ranging from 13 to 14 inches in length. It is difficult to tell franklin's and laughing gulls apart. There are white spots on the outer black wing tips of franklin's gulls but these are hard to see.

Franklin's gulls breed in the prairie regions of the interior of North America from southeast Alberta, southern Saskatchewan, and Manitoba to eastern Oregon, southern Montana, Utah, the

Dakotas, and south to Iowa. They gather into immense flocks in the fall and wander about the plains. They are one of the few gull species that remain inland in large numbers during the winter. But many migrate to the Gulf Coast or to the west coast of South America. They are the only North American gulls that winter far south of the Equator.

### Bonaparte's Gull — *Larus philadelphia*

Bonaparte's gulls may be found in almost all parts of the North American continent during different seasons of the year. They breed in the timbered regions from western Alaska through Canada to west central Ontario, and south to central British Columbia and southeast Alberta. In the fall and winter, these 10-inch-long gulls drift along the coasts, Atlantic and Pacific, toward the south and to the Gulf of Mexico. They also remain on open water in the interior of the United States.

The outer wing tips on bonaparte's gulls are white with black edges. The rest of the wings and back are gray. These gulls have reddish-colored legs.

*During the winter the black head of the bonaparte's gull becomes white with black flecks. This bonaparte's gull is beginning to regrow its black hood in preparation for the breeding season.*

*An adult kittiwake, one of the few species of gulls that don't nest on the ground, stands on its nest on a cliff ledge.*

### LITTLE GULL — *Larus minutus*

Europe and Asia are the home of the little gull, a 10-inch-long member of the Laridae. Little gulls breed in the more northern parts of Europe and Asia, then move south in the fall. During the winter they are found in Great Britain, the Baltic Sea coasts, around the Mediterranean, Black, and Caspian seas, and sometimes in the northeastern United States.

Little gulls have gray backs and wings, with a narrow white edge along the lower part of the wings. Legs and bills are red.

### IVORY GULL — *Pogophila eburnea*

The ivory gull is a circumpolar breeder. These 18-inch-long gulls are found in small scattered groups nesting throughout the Arctic Circle on islands such as Spitsbergen and Franz Josef Land. They winter from the northern drift ice to along the northern coast of North America and Europe, sometimes coming as far south as the United States. They are also found in southern Greenland, Iceland, Norway, and Great Britain in the winter.

Ivory gulls are one of the few all white gulls. Their legs and bills are black and there is a yellow tip on the bill.

### COMMON KITTIWAKE — *Rissa tridactyla*

Another circumpolar breeder, the 18-inch-long kittiwake, is about the size of a ring-billed gull. With the coming of winter, kittiwakes move south to Japan, the northern United States, northern Africa, and along the coasts of the Mediterranean Sea.

Kittiwakes look very similar to laughing gulls. They may be identified by the definite triangular shape of the black on the wing tips and the slightly forked tail.

*Preening the feathers under the wing takes some tricky movements.*

# III

## Plumage and Soft-part Colors

The flight of a gull is a lovely and fascinating sight. The birds appear as graceful white specks in the sky, moving easily with the wind, or against it. They wing their way upward until they are out of sight, or they glide along close to the surface of the water. They are often seen soaring on the updrafts off the edges of beaches, buildings, and bridges.

### PLUMAGE

Feathers enable gulls to fly, and they also provide protection for the birds, just as clothes do for humans. Caring for its feathers takes up a large part of the gull's day and involves preening, oiling, bathing, shaking, and even dusting them with dirt. When a feather becomes disarranged, a gull will usually preen it immediately, because keeping the feathers in good condition is of primary importance to health. Gulls preen mainly while in their daily loafing areas or just after arriving at the roost for the night.

Gulls preen each feather by nibbling it with the bill. The intricate structure of the feather helps keep water away from the bird's body and also controls the temperature of the body. At the base of the gull's tail is a gland called the uropygeal gland. This gland produces an oil that, when rubbed on the feathers, helps to shed water. Without the oil, the bird's feathers would easily become wet.

When birds lose their old, worn-out feathers and grow new ones, this is called molting. Gulls molt twice a year, in the fall and in the spring. Like hair, feathers are dead tissue. They are extremely strong for their light weight and delicate structure,

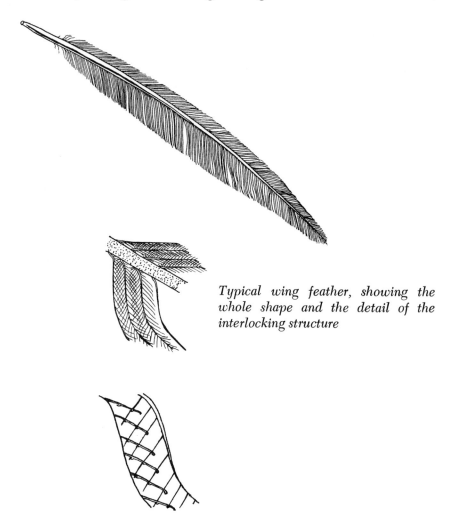

*Typical wing feather, showing the whole shape and the detail of the interlocking structure*

*After their feathers are taken care of, gulls can spend time loafing.*

but they do become worn and broken. Molt always occurs in a specific pattern, a few feathers at a time. All the feathers are not shed at the same time because then the birds would have no protection from the weather and could not fly.

The sequence of molt begins soon after a gull hatches and it continues throughout life. Chicks hatch with a thick covering of soft, fluffy down. At this time in the life of a gull, most of the species appear to be similar in size and coloring. The head and back of the chicks are light brown to buff colored, spotted with dark brown and black. Their underparts are tan to grayish. Glaucous and ivory-gull chicks are pure white, and a few other species are white with brown and black spots. The chicks are

*A day-old chick hides in its nest. It is protected from predators because it blends so well with its surroundings.*

cryptically colored, meaning that they blend into their surroundings. This provides protection as predators have difficulty finding the chicks.

A couple of weeks after hatching, gull chicks begin to grow their first flight feathers, or juvenal plumage. These plumages, like those of the newly hatched chicks, are also similar in most gull species. The young gulls are brown with buff, black, and gray spots. Five to seven weeks after hatching, the chicks have grown their complete juvenal plumage and are able to fly.

The smaller species, such as bonaparte's, franklin's, and little gulls, develop their adult plumage by the time they are two years old. Larger species, such as glaucous, great black-backed, and herring gulls, take three to four years. Under normal conditions, gulls do not begin to breed until they have their complete adult plumage. The typical adult gull has a gray back and

*The parent gull fluffs its feathers and shades its chick.*

*These herring gulls are only a few months old and still have their juvenal plumage.*

wings while the rest of the body is white. Of course there are many variations between species just as there are variations between the different races of people in the world. Some species have a black band across the tail and others have black markings on the wing tips. The pattern of black on the wings is different in each species and is often used for identification.

There is a seasonal change in the adult plumage of some gull species. In early spring the white head feathers of laughing, bonaparte's, franklin's, and little gulls are lost and replaced by black ones. These species are often referred to as black-headed gulls because of this. Most other types of gulls retain the white head during the breeding season in spring and summer. The black-headed gulls molt the black head feathers during the fall molt and replace them with white again.

The time during the year when gulls molt is controlled to some extent by the temperature and length of day, but the main reason that molt occurs when it does is because of energy needs. Raising young and molting each requires a lot of energy. Gulls cannot do both at the same time, so it is not until the breeding season is over in late summer that the adults undergo a complete molt, replacing all the feathers. This prepares them for the cold winter to come. In this way the gulls can use their energy for one purpose at a time. During the spring and summer they raise young, during the fall they molt, and during the winter they keep warm.

*By their third year, herring gulls have grown many of the gray back and wing feathers of an adult.*

*The head and neck of the adult herring gulls become speckled with brown feathers in the fall and winter. During the spring and summer, the head and neck are pure white.*

With the coming of spring the adults undergo a partial molt. Only some of the body feathers are replaced at this time. Now they are again ready to raise young. In the world of the gull, everything is timed so the gulls can go about the job of raising a family most efficiently.

### SOFT PARTS

Ornithologists call the legs, feet, eyes, and bill of a bird the "soft parts." Gull chicks hatch with black or dark brown soft parts. These colors change as the chick matures. As we have seen, not all adult gulls have the same soft-part colors. Some have yellow bills, some have yellow bills with red or black markings, others have all black bills, and still others have all red bills. The legs and feet of the different species vary from black, to gray, to yellow, to flesh colored. These soft-part colors change or intensify prior to the breeding season. This helps the gulls to attract mates.

The closest relatives of birds in the animal kingdom are reptiles and it is from the scales of the primitive ancestral reptiles that feathers evolved. Feathers are the main characteristic used to classify an animal as a bird. With their feathers, the first birds could take to the sky. They no longer had to depend solely on their legs for transportation. This great freedom of flight has fascinated man for centuries as he tried to mimic the birds. The wonders of the gulls' world must be many and varied as the birds view all from their lofty height.

*In the spring, this laughing gull's bill will become bright red. The red color gradually fades back to black during the summer. Scientists believe that the bright bill color helps the gulls to attract mates in the spring.*

# IV

## Food and Feeding Habits

Among the first sounds announcing daybreak at the seashore are the challenge cries of the gulls as they begin their feeding trips for the day. They have left their night roost and are ready for foraging. Feeding can be a loud, raucous affair as the gulls jealously guard or fight over bits of food. They usually settle their disputes by screeching and wing-flapping, with no physical contact. Mealtime is not always noisy, though. If only a few gulls are feeding together, they may walk along quietly, each intent only on its own business. Feeding activity alternates with loafing throughout the day, until at dusk the birds return to their roosts for the night.

The great versatility of the gulls is seen best in their feeding habits. They are opportunists when it comes to mealtime, finding and using many different types of food—fish, insects, garbage, anything that will provide them with energy. Their ability to exploit various food sources enables them to live almost everywhere in the world.

Contrary to popular belief, most gulls do not depend on catching live fish for a major part of their diet. When they do fish, they don't dive into the water as pelicans and terns do. They hover close to the surface and reach quickly into the water with their bills to snatch the prey. Gulls eat sardines, pin fish, or bait fish—almost anything small enough to swallow.

Gulls may eat shellfish, such as clams, but before they can eat a clam they must open the shell. To do this, the gull picks up the clam, flies into the air, and drops it. If the shell hits something hard, it will break and the gull has a meal, if he can swoop down to get it before a watchful neighbor does. If the shell drops on sand, the gull must pick it up and try again.

During low tide, many gulls feed on sand bars and mud banks. They walk along picking up anything that looks edible, sometimes washing bits of food before eating them. The gulls eat marine worms and small crustaceans as well as dead fish and other refuse cast up by the tide. Some things, such as jellyfish, have little food value and are left alone. Off and on, while walking slowly along the shore, a gull will stop to preen or chase away a neighbor that gets too close.

*Meandering over the piles of debris in a garbage dump, laughing gulls look for something edible.*

*Laughing gulls follow along trying to steal fish from the hard-working pelicans. Often one of the gulls will land on the back or head of a pelican while waiting for its chance.*

A funny thing that laughing gulls try to do is steal food from brown pelicans. A feeding flock of pelicans almost always is followed by a group of laughing gulls. The gulls do not dive for fish themselves but wait for a pelican to surface after a catch. Then, quick as a flash, they light on its head or back and wait for an opportunity to snatch a morsel. They rarely get anything from the pelicans, who don't seem to mind the passengers.

Foot-paddling is thought to be another method by which gulls feed. The gulls stand in one or two inches of water and move their feet up and down as though they were mashing something. This stirs up the sand and may cause some crustaceans and mollusks to come to the surface, where the gulls can catch them. Some individuals do not feed on what they stir up by foot-paddling, however. They simply paddle for a few minutes and then go on to some other activity. Ornithologists are not sure why gulls foot-paddle. Gulls are among the most well-studied birds in the world and yet many aspects of their daily lives still remain a mystery.

Some gulls, such as great black-backs, herring, and western, eat the eggs and young of other species of gulls and other birds. They only do this when the eggs or young are left unprotected. An intruder entering a nesting colony causes tremendous damage. Parent birds leave their nests to escape the potential danger and the less fearful gulls move in to feed on the eggs and helpless young.

California, ring-billed, franklin's, and bonaparte's gulls spend all or part of the year inland. Here, they eat worms, mice, insects, and grasshoppers. When farmers plow their fields, a flock of gulls will follow along behind. Farmers are almost always glad to see the gulls because the birds eat many harmful pests turned up by the plow. The agile gulls can also catch insects out of the air.

In 1848, the crops of some Mormon settlers in the West were being eaten by thousands of grasshoppers. No matter how hard the Mormons tried to fight off the harmful insects, it did no good. There were two or three grasshoppers on every head of grain, consuming whole fields of crops in minutes. Then one day a flock of gulls arrived and began to eat the pests. So greedily did the gulls feed that they often stopped to regurgitate what they had just eaten, and then ate more. Day after day the gulls returned, until the plague was gone.

Once in a while, though, gulls are not so helpful. Gulls have been known to eat grain just planted by farmers, but they rarely do this.

People tend to think gulls lead romantic lives, probably because they associate the gulls with the sea. This is far from the truth. For a gull, life is a constant search for food. Greedy scavengers, they often find their food in places where man dumps his

*Taking a loafing break after feeding in the dump below, these gulls rest or preen until they are ready to feed again.*

refuse. Dirty harbors, fishing piers, and garbage dumps are favorite feeding places.

However, gulls do man a great service in their scavenging. They help keep beaches and harbors clean. A large population of gulls in an area eats enormous quantities of food each day. Without the gulls, this organic material would rot on shores and in harbors.

Through open garbage dumps, man has allowed the huge increase in gull populations in recent years. Each year as the human population grows, more garbage is thrown away, providing more food for the gulls. In years when their natural food is not abundant, gulls resort to feeding on human debris and survive.

Another place gulls are often found feeding is at sewage outfalls—places where sewage is disposed of by piping it out into a large body of water. The helpful gulls almost seem to be trying to clean up human pollution.

At the seashore, feeding gulls is a favorite pastime of many people, young and old. Picnickers along the coasts have no trouble collecting a great flock of hungry gulls by throwing a few scraps of food into the air. At times, the gulls are brave enough to take food right from a person's hand. People riding in ferries across bays and harbors frequently attract a following of gulls by feeding them from the stern of the boat.

Coastal gulls follow in the wake of ships and fishing boats as the vessels come and go on their sea journeys. When the ships' cooks throw fish scraps or garbage overboard, the gulls swoop down to feed. Often the gulls don't land on the water but pick up the desired morsel and are off again without wetting a feather. Fishermen are old friends of the gulls. Coming in from a day on the water, the sportsmen stop to clean their catch before going home, and the raucous gulls snatch up every discarded scrap. Often two gulls will fight over a particular bit and

*Flying off with a scrap, a young herring gull escapes his comrades to eat in peace.*

a tug-of-war follows. The winner flies off a short distance to eat his bite in peace. As the fishermen finish their chore, the hoarse screeches and cries of the feeding gulls subside.

Garbage scows are another favorite of the gulls. As the scows ply to and from the harbors, hundreds of gulls follow or ride along while feeding.

Gulls can drink either fresh or salt water. They have special glands in the head that remove excess salt from their blood after they drink salt water. This salt is then secreted from the nares, the holes in the gull's upper mandible. However, given a choice, gulls prefer fresh water. It makes less work for their bodies not to have to remove the salt.

The gulls' diet varies with their locality and what is obtainable. If one type of food is not available, then they find another. Their scavenging methods are haphazard and careless. Gulls will try to eat almost anything. In dumps they walk over the piles of trash, picking up whatever catches their eye, throwing some things away and eating others.

The problem is that the gulls' lack of pickiness about what they eat often gets them into trouble. There are numerous known instances of a gull being killed by what it ate. One gull swallowed a live mole, which then bit through the gull's esophagus in trying to escape. The gull died and the mole never got

*Pools of water, even in parking lots, provide a drink for gulls. They can drink salt water but seem to prefer fresh water.*

*A group of bird watchers saved this almost mature great black-back from drowning in Pelham Bay, New York. They nursed the gull back to health and later released it in the same area.*

out. An autopsy on another dead gull showed two razor blades in its stomach. They had severely cut it.

Frequently a gull will become hopelessly entangled in line or severely hooked as it feeds around fishermen at piers. When a fisherman accidentally hooks a gull and then cuts the line to get rid of the bird, a length of fishing line is left trailing on the gull. Returning to its colony, the gull will become entangled in the bushes and die of starvation. The fisherman who snares a bird can save its life by reeling it in and removing the hook and line.

Gulls are clever in some ways but seem very stupid in others. They have learned that fishing piers are good places to find food, but they have not learned to avoid the hooks and lines. They know garbage dumps provide easy meals, but they are not choosy about what they eat. Yet, in spite of the fact that gulls make some not very intelligent choices, they seem to know what they need to in order to survive.

41

# V

# Courtship and Nest Building

Spring comes heralded by the return of the gulls to their nesting grounds. This return is gradual and it may take several weeks for all of the birds to gather at the old colony site. The colony may be located amidst clumps of grasses surrounding a pond, on a sandy island in a gulf, or between rocks and bushes along a shore. Some gulls have even been known to nest on large, flat rooftops and on the ledges of buildings.

As the first few gulls make their way back from their wintering area, they are seen loafing in areas around the colony. With each passing day, more and more gulls gather. During this time the older gulls renew pair bonds with their mates from previous years. The pairs stand close together while the unpaired birds stand singly. Gulls normally mate for life. If one member of a pair dies, the surviving member usually finds another mate.

Gulls that have nested together in previous years are the first ones to move from the loafing areas around the colony into the main nesting area. They seem hesitant at first to land in their old, familiar breeding grounds. The gulls have spent the fall and winter along beaches or in open areas where they had a clear view to watch for danger. In the nesting colony they must settle among bushes, tall weeds, or rocks, which obstruct their

Adult laughing gull arrives at the nesting grounds.

Two pairs of gulls stand on the edge of their colony. They have gone through their courtship rituals and are ready to move into the colony and start building nests.

*Two pairs of laughing gulls displaying early in the breeding season*

view. After quickly landing and taking off several times, a few gulls begin to stay on the ground. Once the first birds have settled, it doesn't take long for the others to follow. For a few days they may stand around in small groups, seeming to be in no hurry to start the business of nest building and laying eggs.

The previously established gull pairs go through courtship quickly and select their nest sites first, often choosing the same area they used the year before. Younger birds, nesting for the first time, or birds that have lost their mates, must perform more extensive courtship ceremonies to find a mate. This goes on while they are standing around in groups in the colony or in the loafing areas nearby. Although it may be impossible for humans to tell the difference between male and female gulls, the gulls have little trouble doing so.

The female usually approaches a male and the two of them walk away from the rest of the group. The male begins tugging at the grasses around him as if to pull them up for nesting material. He may utter a low, melodious, gobbling call as he pulls at the grass. In response, the female may beg for food from the male, lowering her head and looking up at him. She does this in the same way that chicks beg for food from their parents. Or the female may walk around the male, lowering her breast and raising her tail, uttering the gobbling call. The two spend a long time getting to know each other by using these ritual behavior patterns which tell their mood and intentions. Sometimes they rub each others necks until the male finally mounts the female's

*The female gull (left) begs for food from her mate as part of their courtship. Bottom: After a minute or two of begging, the female is fed regurgitated food by the male.*

*A pair of gulls defends their territory from other nearby gulls. Soon they will begin building their nest here.*

back and they copulate. This signifies that the pair is firmly formed and the two adults are ready to cooperate in the effort to raise a family.

Now the pair must choose a nest site and establish territory around it. The older pairs are already well along in the process of nest building, and the new pairs choose nest sites around the established group. For a while they walk about their territory driving away any bird that comes too close. Soon they begin gathering grass, twigs, shells, or moss. These are woven into a well-constructed nest. As the nest takes shape, frequently one of the gulls will sit in it, pushing the sides into shape to form a rounded cup two to four inches deep for the eggs. Nest building usually takes one to two weeks.

The ground-nesting gulls often choose a nest site next to a bush, rock, clump of grass, or other barrier. The cliff-nesting gulls, like kittiwakes, each choose a solitary ledge, and rooftop breeders often build near a chimney or other obstruction. This gives the incubating birds protection on at least one side so they don't have to keep watch all around.

While building a nest, a pair must continue to defend the territory around it. If they are not aggressive enough and insistent about protecting their own space, they will not be successful. Other individuals will intrude and take their territory, their nesting material, or eat their eggs.

If one gull steps into another gull's territory, the owner walks up to the strayed neighbor, stands still and tall, and stares at

*When gulls hold their wings out from the body and drooped down like this, it means they feel aggressive.*

*Territorial defense behavior: A, Upright and staring; and B, Grass pulling*

him. This may scare away the trespasser, or he may just stare back at the owner. When staring doesn't work, the owner may reach down and viciously pull at the grass around him as if to say, "This is what I'll do to you if you don't leave!" After a grass-pulling bout, the intruder usually departs. If he doesn't, violent action may follow. The territory owner rushes at him with wings flapping and begins pecking him. As soon as the intruder is driven away, peace returns. Actual physical contact between adults is more frequent early in the breeding season when territories are first being claimed. Once territory boundaries have been established and neighbors have learned where they belong, there is little fighting. Violence is replaced by more peaceful rituals. A mated pair may do a courtship dance together when another bird comes too near, telling it, "Go away. This is our territory and we are busy with each other." It is rare that an intruder takes over a territory from the owner.

Sometimes after a bird is driven away, the territory owner gives a "trumpet call." Lowering the head and stretching out the neck, the gull gradually raises its neck, giving a series of short, loud calls. The calling gets louder as the head goes up. Finally, with the head as high as possible, a series of short, harsh notes is given and the head is tossed a few times. Nearby gulls may repeat the call, as if to tell the intruder not to come near them either. The trumpet call may be given for no apparent reason by a gull standing alone. This is like a dare—"I dare anyone to try to invade my territory."

*During an unusually fierce disagreement, one gull flies at an intruding neighbor, screeching and pecking.*

*Frequently throughout the period of pair bond formation the pairs copulate. They will continue to do this during nest building also.*

During nest building, the paired gulls continue the courtship rituals, and they copulate frequently. Sometimes the pairs look as if they are dancing with each other as they perform their ritualized behavior displays. These body postures and calls allow the individuals to communicate effectively with one another.

Soon after the nest is completed, the female lays the first egg. Two more eggs usually follow, with one to two days between the laying of each one. Sometimes only one or two eggs are laid, but very rarely more than three. With the arrival of the first egg, the parents take turns staying at the nest to protect it and to maintain the proper temperature for the developing embryo. The hot sun will boil the eggs and cool temperatures will chill them.

Adult gulls have three brood patches. These are areas on the breast where the feathers fall out during the courtship period. The blood vessels near the surface of the skin in these areas enlarge. The adults incubate the eggs next to these brood patches and the closeness of the blood vessels passes warmth to the eggs. Gull eggs develop at temperatures of about 103 degrees, slightly higher than human temperatures. At the end of the breeding season, the feathers grow back on the brood patches. The complete feather coat is necessary for the birds to survive the rigors of winter.

*This laughing-gull nest with its complete clutch of three eggs is well hidden in the surrounding grasses.*

*The parent whose turn it is to incubate the eggs moves in to settle on the nest.*

The brooding parent must sit still hour after hour, keeping the eggs at the correct temperature. Now and then the adult will shift position or give a trumpet call. Frequently it will turn the eggs with its bill so the embryo will develop properly. During the hottest part of the day it stands and shades the eggs from the

*During hot weather the incubating adult fluffs its feathers to allow air to circulate through them. It also pants much as a dog does.*

direct rays of the sun instead of incubating them. When the adults get hot, they ruffle their feathers, allowing air to move around the bases of the feathers and provide cooling. Also, the birds pant, much the way a dog does, to keep cool. When a brooding adult's mate returns to take its turn at watching the nest, the pair may make soft calls to each other. Then the gull on the nest moves off and its partner steps on, adjusts its feathers, and settles to its long chore. The relieved bird may stand around near the nest for some time or it may take off immediately to search for food.

All gull eggs look very similar. They are about the size of a chicken egg, and have a buff or buff-green background with brown and black splotches all over them. These colors make it difficult for a predator to find the eggs. Like the young chicks, eggs are cryptically colored. Much variation exists in the color and markings on the eggs, even between the eggs in one nest.

The incubation period lasts between 22 and 30 days, depending on the species. The adults never seem to tire or get bored with their duties. Night and day, at least one member of the pair is at the nest.

*The parent frequently turns the eggs to insure proper development of the embryos.*

# VI
## Raising a Family

As the time for the eggs to hatch draws near, the adult gulls seem to grow impatient. When a small, weak, peeping sound is heard from within the shell, the incubating adult often stands up and looks down at the egg as if wondering what's going on in there. A day or two after the peeping sounds begin, the egg starts to hatch.

The first egg laid is the first one to hatch and the others follow in two to three days. Just before hatching, a calcium deposit forms on the tip of the chick's bill. This is called the egg tooth. The chick pushes the egg tooth against the inside of the shell to break it open.

Little cracks first appear in the shell near the big end of the egg. Within a day, the chick finally manages to break a small hole in its shell. This is called pipping the egg. Less than a day later the chick pushes off the top of the shell and emerges into the world. One of the parents will soon take the empty shell and fly away with it, because the white inside of the shell is easily visible and could attract a predator.

Chicks arrive in the world worn out from the effort of breaking out of their shells. They are covered with wet down feathers, making them look bedraggled and helpless. In six to ten hours,

*Having broken off the large end of the egg, the baby chick begins to unfold itself.*

*A day-old chick rests on top of one of its siblings which has just pipped its egg.*

however, the down is dry and it is hard to believe that such a fluffy ball ever came out of its small shell.

A definite change occurs in the behavior of the adults when their eggs hatch. The colony becomes more active and noisy. For a month the adults have had little to do but incubate eggs and feed themselves. Now they must feed an additional one to three hungry stomachs. The new chicks will almost double in weight every five or six days during their first month of life.

Only a few hours after hatching, chicks begin to beg for food

*This four-day-old chick is begging for food from its parent.*

from their parents. They poke at the adults' bills, giving a plaintive, cheeping call. The poking and cheeping induces the parents to regurgitate food, which is dropped onto the nest. The

*A newly hatched laughing gull, still damp from the egg*

adult gulls must pick it up and offer it directly to the chicks.
The nestlings soon learn what food is, where it comes from, and
where it is supposed to go. After a few days of being handed the
food, the chicks learn to pick it up from the nest by themselves.
Often they become so greedy that they grab the food right from
the parents' bills.

During the first few days of life, chicks spend all their time
either eating or sleeping. They wake up, beg, eat, and fall asleep
immediately, as if exhausted from the effort. Any regurgitated
food that the chicks leave is eaten again by the parents. Food is
valuable, and the adults have to work hard to catch enough for
their growing brood and themselves. No morsel is wasted.

Each day the newborn chicks grow and become more active.
Their wobbly legs gradually become stronger and soon they are

walking about outside their nests. At first they spend considerable time picking themselves up from falls. It takes practice to develop coordinated muscles.

Just as they protected the eggs, one or both of the adults will stay at the nest all the time to protect the young chicks. Fish crows, other gulls, or small mammals will eat the defenseless chicks if they are left alone. When the adults are disturbed by an intruder in the colony, usually a human but sometimes a fox or dog, they fly away, giving a loud alarm call that sounds like *"Gah-gah-gah! Gah-gah-gah!"* The young chicks, hearing this call, automatically crouch down and remain motionless. With their camouflaged plumage, they are almost impossible to see.

*When an adult gull is frightened away from its nest by an intruder, it leaves its eggs and young unprotected. The cryptic coloration of eggs and chicks helps to protect them.*

*These siblings are in the process of losing their down and growing their first flight feathers or juvenal plumage.*

Older chicks that can run well head for the nearest hiding spot when the alarm call sounds. The adults fly in circles overhead and sometimes dive at the intruder to force him away. One of the authors was actually knocked to the ground by an adult great black-backed gull that dived at him in a colony.

Parents must also protect the chicks from temperature fluctuations. Chicks cannot regulate their own body temperatures until they are at least a week old. As the chicks begin to stay awake for longer periods of time, they occasionally peek out from under the brooding parent to get a look at the world. When the temperature is not too hot or too cold for the chicks, the parent may stand beside the nest.

Chicks begin to preen their feathers almost as soon as they can stand up. They bend their heads down and try to reach the breast feathers, but that is too much balancing for them at first and—*plop*—over they fall. Undaunted, the chicks continue to try to preen various parts of their bodies and within a couple of weeks they become quite proficient at it.

*An adult gull doing the wing-leg stretch, a comfort movement, which chicks also do.*

Once the chicks are able to walk they begin to explore their surroundings. The inquisitive young pick up and play with any objects they find around the nest, especially twigs, leaves, and shells. They practice flapping and stretching their wings. They do the wing-leg stretch that their parents do, stretching one wing and leg behind them. They try to do all the things that their parents do, and slowly they learn how. If they wander too far from the nest while learning and exploring, their parents call them back.

As the nesting season progresses, the chicks need less attention and both parents stay away from the nest for longer periods throughout the day. The adult gulls must spend more of their time finding food for the young now, because chicks need to eat

*Two young chicks explore the area around their nest under the watchful eye of their parents.*

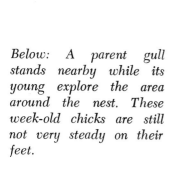

*A pair of laughing gulls standing near their nest with their six-day-old chick*

*Below: A parent gull stands nearby while its young explore the area around the nest. These week-old chicks are still not very steady on their feet.*

more as they grow to adulthood.

A parent returning to the colony always lands near its own nest. If its chicks are not there, the adult will call to them. The chicks head toward the familiar voice from their hiding place in the cool shade of a nearby bush. A returning parent usually has been out fishing and is ready to feed its hungry offspring. The young chicks crouch low and begin peeping and poking at the parent's bill. It is amazing how a large chick can make itself appear small and submissive at meal time! The hungry chicks are very insistent in their begging. They eagerly reach toward the parent's bill and grab the food as it is regurgitated.

Feeding can be a rough time for parent gulls as their chicks grow larger. They get pecked, poked, and shoved as their young grab for food. Once an adult has regurgitated all the food it has for its ill-mannered chicks, it often leaves the area immediately. All that pushing and shoving must annoy the parents at times.

Healthy gull chicks are a little larger and heavier than their parents by the time they are five to six weeks old. They have almost grown their complete juvenal plumage and spend considerable time flapping their wings and preening. Most gulls learn to fly between five and seven weeks of age. The first real flight that takes them away from their nest is called fledging. The smaller species fledge at a younger age than do the larger species.

The young gulls almost seem reluctant to leave the security of

*Upon returning to its nest, an adult is immediately besieged by one of its hungry chicks.*

*Fledglings gather on the beach around their colony, exercising their wings and practicing short flights in preparation for leaving home.*

home after they first learn to fly. They spend a couple of weeks standing with other young, and adults, around the edges of the colony, frequently returning to their own nest to be fed by their parents. The hesitant chicks don't venture far from the colony. It takes them a while to develop their flight abilities.

As the nesting season draws to a close and they no longer need their parents to take care of them, the young gulls begin to go farther and farther from home. While being fed by their parents, the chicks stored up lots of fat against these days when they must learn to feed themselves. This is not easy to do and during the learning period their bodies live on the extra fat. At first, the youngsters depend on following the more experienced birds to find food sources, but gradually they become independent.

The once active and noisy gull colony becomes quiet. There are no more territories to defend. Slowly, everyone is leaving, the young and the adults. Few traces of the wonders that took place here are left. A few feathers blow about in the breeze and a chill in the air signifies the coming of winter. A new generation of gulls is out in the world learning about soaring, and catching fish, and the other things that gulls do.

# VII

## Relatives of the Gulls

Ornithologists classify the gulls and their relatives in the Order Charadriiformes, which includes shorebirds, gulls, terns, and auks. The Order is divided into three suborders. Shorebirds, such as knots and sandpipers, are included in the Suborder Charadrii. The Suborder Alcae includes the auks, murres, and puffins. The gulls and their closest relatives are in the Suborder Lari.

There are three families in the gull's suborder: (1) Family Stercoradriidae—skuas and jaegers, (2) Family Laridae—gulls and terns, (3) Family Rynchopidae—skimmers. This classification is based on similarities and differences in structure and behavior of the different birds. Species are more closely related to other members of their same family than they are to members of another family.

### Family Stercoradriidae

To Americans, jaegers and skuas are different species of birds belonging to the same family. In Britain all the species of Stercoradriidae are referred to as skuas. This is a good example of why scientific names are so important and common names so confusing. The Latin name of a bird (or any plant or animal

*An adult skua defends its territory from other birds. Skuas are more aggressive than most gulls.*

species) is the same the world over. As scientists study a species, they may learn that they classified it incorrectly and change its Latin name but this is done by general agreement.

Jaegers and skuas are larger than most gulls and their back plumage is dark brown rather than gray. Some have patches of white on the wings and the belly is all white. The bill is gull-like but has a more strongly hooked tip. The claws are more hooked and sharper than gulls'. The feet are never used to hold prey, in spite of the strong talons. The legs are short and strong. The wings are longer and more pointed than gulls' wings, making their flight resemble that of a hawk.

Young jaegers and skuas fish like gulls, but as they mature they become active birds of prey. They are much more aggressive than gulls; in fact, they act like hawks and falcons. They are well known for their habit of chasing and pestering other sea birds until the plagued ones drop their meal. The skua or jaeger then swoops down quickly and snaps up the food before it can reach the water. They must be quick and agile to do this.

When not breeding, jaegers and skuas fly out over the sea without landing for days. At sea they are primarily loners. Often one or two will follow a ship, waiting for garbage to be thrown overboard. The young probably stay at sea most of the time until they are three to four years old and ready to breed. They are truly pelagic sea birds, meaning that they spend most of their time off shore. They lead very different lives from gulls and are rarely seen with their gull relatives.

Upon returning to their breeding grounds in the spring, jaegers and skuas become vocal and aggressive. They breed in colonies, like gulls. Any intruder, man or animal, is attacked fiercely by these dive-bombing birds. Other species of birds and their young are attacked and eaten by the jaegers and skuas. Eggs are another source of food for them.

They build their nests on the ground, leaving large spaces between neighbors. The nesting area is frequently near other bird colonies, which the jaegers and skuas use as food sources. Their nests are just a scrape in the ground that barely resembles a nest. The eggs, usually two, are earth colored with dull green and gray blotches. Both sexes share the incubation duties, as well as the feeding and care of the young. The breeding range of jaegers and skuas is bipolar. This means that they breed in both arctic and antarctic regions. They are long-distance migrants and may fly as far as the tropics during the winter. Some follow the coasts while migrating and others stay far out at sea.

### FAMILY LARIDAE

Terns, which are in the gulls' same family, have a world-wide distribution. Those nesting in the colder climates either stay near the coastline or near inland bodies of water. Those living in the warmer climates venture far out to sea, nesting on oceanic islands. Terns are generally smaller and more slender than gulls and have a forked tail. Most terns have gray backs while the rest of their plumage is white, but there are some all white terns. Many terns have black crown feathers that in some species are lost during the winter. The bill is more slender than a gull's bill and is straight on the tip.

Terns are remarkably gregarious, nesting in vast colonies. They are usually seen feeding in groups, and flying together, too, but they seldom land in the water and swim, although they have webbed feet. Terns spend more time in the air than do gulls. They do not walk around garbage dumps and along beaches searching for food. When feeding, terns plunge from the air and catch their prey just below the surface of the water. They are the only true divers in the Order Charadriiformes. Some terns feed on insects that they catch in the air.

*This royal tern shows the close similarities between gulls and terns.*

Nesting is preceded by lovely aerial displays in which a pair of terns dart around very close together. There is also courtship feeding as with the gulls. One to four eggs are laid, depending on the species of tern. The eggs are grayish with ashy or brown blotches. Young terns take two to as many as seven or eight years to mature and begin breeding.

When an intruder comes into a tern colony, some species will make bold, threatening dives and even strike the intruder. Other terns simply fly away when disturbed.

## FAMILY RYNCHOPIDAE

The skimmers are perhaps the most distant relatives in the gulls' suborder. They get their name from their unique feeding habits. Their lower mandible, or jaw, which is flattened sideways, can be lowered to a 45° angle. The bird flies along just above the surface of the water, with the lower mandible knifing through the water. Because of its thinness, the mandible offers little resistance to the water and does not slow the bird down. When the lower mandible strikes a fish or shrimp, the bird's head snaps forward and the upper mandible closes on the prey.

Skimmers often feed at sunset, especially when the water is calm. They skim along, disturbing the tiny plant or animal life in the water. These small organisms glow when disturbed. This glow can attract small fish and other forms of aquatic life, if the sun is not too bright. The skimmers then retrace their path and collect the curious fish that have responded to the glow.

In proportion to their bodies, skimmers' wings are longer and wider than gulls'. Their bills are straight with no hook on the tip, and the lower mandible is longer than the upper one. Their wings, back, neck and the back of their heads are black. Their underparts are all white.

Black skimmers breed colonially all along the southeastern United States Atlantic and Gulf coasts. Other species of skim-

*A pair of black skimmers guard their nest. Notice the chick sleeping under the breast of the brooding adult.*

mers live in Africa, India, and Burma. Their colonies are found on sand bars and open beaches, often in areas that are susceptible to disturbance by humans or very high tides. Their nests are scrapes in the sand, like many tern nests. One to four eggs are laid. These are slightly glossy and stone colored, with brown and gray blotches.

Skimmers usually do not attack intruders in their colonies. They fly overhead waiting until they can safely return to their nests. Young skimmers are sand colored at first and blend in very well with the sand on the beaches. Skimmers are probably one of the least studied birds of the Order Charadriiformes.

These are the closest relatives of the gulls. Note their many similarities in behavior and appearance. All these birds have

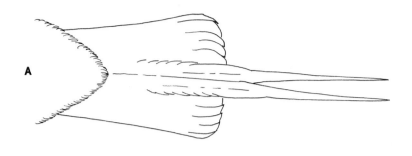

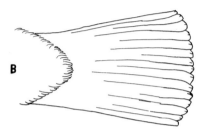

*Comparison of the tails of: A, skua; B, gull; and C, tern*

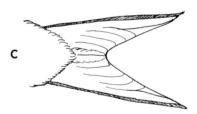

webbed feet with three toes connected in the web. They are all colonial nesters, building their nests on the ground or on cliffs or, rarely, in bushes. Their eggs and young are cryptically colored. Both male and female have similar plumage and the female is sometimes smaller than the male. They live near either fresh water lakes or salt water. For these reasons and many more, these birds are grouped together by scientists.

# VIII
## Men and Gulls

Bird that dwellest in the spray,
White as yon moon's calm array,
Dust thy beauty ne'er may stain.
Sunbeam gauntlet of the main!
Soaring with aerial motion
On the surges of the ocean.
                    (*Welsh 1325–85?*)

Gulls have been immensely popular with writers and artists for centuries. No other bird evokes the image of romance so strongly. In poetry and paintings, gulls are associated with freedom, grace, and beauty. They are pictured as dainty creatures soaring gracefully out to sea, oblivious to all that goes on below. Long envied by man for their freedom, gulls seem to lead the ideal life. The very popular *Jonathan Livingston Seagull*, by Richard Bach, furthered the image of this bird. In this book, Jonathan was a gull searching for happiness and a purpose in life, much as a person does.

However, gulls do not really lead such romantic lives, as we have seen. They are greedy scavengers, eating refuse and inhabiting places that many other birds cannot. The reasons for the

71

*Gracefully, a laughing gull soars along with its feet extended behind it.*

"mystique" of the gulls are not known. Perhaps it is man's yearning for the power of flight, or his desire to be associated with the sea as closely as some gulls are. Men and gulls are tied together by more than just poetry and paintings, though. They play important roles in each others' lives.

Man has caused many problems for the gulls. Prior to the 1900's, gulls eggs were a great source of food. Men would visit a colony every day and collect all the eggs. By doing this, they could be sure of getting fresh eggs each day. The "frustrated" gulls, finding their nests empty, would lay again. In the early 1900's, some people realized that this continual nest-robbing would destroy the gull populations. Soon there would be no more eggs for people to eat. Laws were passed that no eggs could be taken after July 4 each year. The gulls were allowed to raise any eggs laid after this date. Today no egging is allowed at all. Several species of gulls were almost eradicated before this practice was stopped.

Young gulls were also considered good eating. Chicks were taken from the colony before they could fly and fattened up at home for a month or two. Then they were cooked like chicken. This was outlawed along with the taking of eggs.

Not all of man's activities have been bad for the gulls. As man develops an area, the gulls move into it with him. Parking lots and large rooftops provide loafing, roosting, and nesting spots for the social gulls. Garbage dumps and other refuse-disposal areas provide the necessary food sources. At times one could almost imagine the gulls are waiting for man's next move.

But man also destroys some of the places that gulls need. He builds houses on nesting colony areas. He pollutes waters so that no fish are available for the gulls. So far, some gulls have been able to adapt to the disruptive changes. In a few cases they have been able to increase in numbers because of human activities, especially where man has increased food availability.

Gulls also cause problems for man. One of the greatest is that

*The romantic image of gulls is quickly dispelled by a visit to a garbage dump. Here the scavengers greedily search for edible scraps.*

of gulls on airport runways. The wide open spaces of the runways provide ideal loafing spots for the gulls. An airplane taking off or landing may strike the resting gulls and ruin the plane's engines or even crash.

Some airports have trouble with gulls and some do not. Scientists studying aircraft-bird strikes have discovered that the airports with gull problems are located near a food source for the gulls, such as a dirty harbor or garbage dump. A fresh water source nearby also attracts the gulls, since the birds must drink after feeding. Logan Airport, in Boston, Massachusetts, has had numerous incidences of planes hitting gulls in past years. Thousands of herring gulls feed on the garbage in the dumps surrounding Boston Harbor. The gulls then fly to an open area, after feeding, to spend time loafing, preening, and sleeping. The nearest open area where they can do this is Logan Airport.

Once the pesky gulls have chosen a loafing spot, it is hard to get rid of them. Many techniques have been and are being tried to keep them away from airports but none has really succeeded. Loud gun blasts broadcast over the runways scare the gulls away for awhile, but the birds soon adapt to the noise and ignore it. Driving a car on the runways between plane flights would keep the gulls from settling down, but this would require several cars and hiring several extra people at large airports. The best solutions are not to build airports next to the sea and not to locate garbage dumps near existing airports.

Man has tried to put gulls to work for him at times. There has been some speculation about the possible use of gulls in detecting submarines damaged in conflict during a war. It was thought that if the submarine released food, any gulls in the area would be attracted to it, thus revealing the location of the damaged submarine. This possibility was not pursued because most submarine attacks are out at sea and gulls are shorebirds. They do not usually fly far out over the ocean.

74

*Gulls glide in, looking for a place to land, and join the large throng feeding at a garbage dump.*

*A large flock of young and adult ring-billed gulls takes flight. Gulls help*

Gulls' feeding habits have been immeasurably useful in other ways, however. As we have seen, without their local gull populations, many harbors would be much more clogged with debris than they are. Also, farmers would have many more insects to contend with than they do. So man and gulls seem to be able to

*keep our beaches clean by eating debris that washes in to shore.*

help each other live in this changing world.

Each year scientists spend many hours working in various gull colonies throughout the world. They want to learn more about gulls—where they go, what they eat, how long they live, and numerous other things. To help in obtaining this information, the scientists band young gulls before they learn to fly. Each chick in a colony is caught and an aluminum Fish and Wildlife Service Band is placed on one of its legs. The number on each chick's band is different from any other band number. The band also says, "Advise Fish and Wildlife Service, Washington, D.C." Anyone who finds a band or a banded bird is requested to send the band number to the Fish and Wildlife Service. Then the Service writes to the scientist who banded that bird and tells

*Aluminum United States Fish and Wildlife Service bird band. Anyone finding a band is asked to report it to the Fish and Wildlife Service in Washington, D.C. This helps the ornithologists who are studying the birds.*

*This herring-gull chick's leg has just been banded. By following the movements of banded birds, scientists can learn more about them.*

78

*A laughing gull surveys its world, wary of man, yet deriving benefits from his presence.*

him when and where the bird was found. In this way, much valuable information is collected about the gulls' lives.

Sometimes when the gulls are banded, a colored plastic streamer is put on next to the aluminum band. This makes the banded gull more easily visible, especially from a distance.

Banding gulls may help to find solutions to the gull-airport problem. It could also help to discover if gulls are potential disease carriers. Band recoveries enable scientists to trace the movement patterns and habits of gulls. Then, if need be, the gulls' movements can be interrupted or changed to some extent. Perhaps the greatest benefit from banding gulls is that man can add to his general knowledge about his environment.

The more we know about the world in which we live, the better prepared we are to make decisions about how to protect that world.

# Index